Quotes on
Life, Goal and Success from
famous people around the world

**Sneha Rawat**

# Introduction

This book is a collection of the most powerful words ever used by the greatest minds around the world. It contains the best of the wisdom they got during their lives. Words have power. Admit it or not words can make you feel the happiest man on earth or the saddest person ever lived. The whole law of attraction theory revolves around the power of words.

As Tony Robbins says, Words have the power to start wars or create peace, destroy relationships or strengthen them. How we feel about anything is shaped by the meaning we attach to it. The words you consciously or unconsciously select to describe a situation immediately change what it means to you and thus how you feel.

"Language shapes our behavior, and each word we use is imbued with multitudes of personal meaning. The right words spoken in the right way can bring us love, money, and respect, while the wrong words—or even the right words spoken in the wrong way—can lead to a country to war. We must carefully orchestrate our speech if we want to achieve our goals and bring our dreams to fruition."
—Dr. Andrew Newberg, Words Can Change Your Brain

Throughout human history, great leaders have used the power of words to transform our emotions, to enlist us in their causes, and to shape the course of destiny.

As Jim Rohn always said there are five major pieces of life: Philosophy, Attitude, Activity, Result, and Lifestyle.

And to create any change in life, you must start by refining your philosophy. You cannot change your destination overnight, but you can change your direction overnight.

These quotes are collected in such a way that they will help you to refine your philosophy.

Start each day with a powerful word of wisdom and let it guide you to take action, overcome fear, boost your self-esteem, create success.

There is no better than adversity.
Every defeat, every heartbreak,
every loss, contains its own seed, its
own lesson on how to improve your
performance the next time.
— Malcolm X

"Dream as if you'll live forever, live as if you'll die today."
— James Dean


"...God's love is so real that He created you to prove it."
— Nick Vujicic, Life Without Limits


"Impossible is just a word thrown around by small men who find it easier to live in the world they've been given than to explore the power they have to change it. Impossible is not a fact. It's an opinion. Impossible is potential. Impossible is temporary. Impossible is nothing."
— Muhammad Ali

"Courage is the discovery that you may not win, and trying when you know you can lose."
— Tom Krause

"Nobody can go back and start a new beginning, but anyone can start today and make a new ending."
— Maria Robinson

"Setting goals is the first step in turning the invisible into the visible."
— Tony Robbins

"Success is simple. Do what's right, the right way, at the right time."
— Arnold H. Glasgow

"Life is full of beauty. Notice it. Notice the bumble bee, the small child, and the smiling faces. Smell the rain, and feel the wind. Live your life to the fullest potential, and fight for your dreams."
— Ashley Smith


"If you have built castles in the air, your work need not be lost; that is where they should be. Now put the foundations under them."
— Henry David Thoreau


"Victory is sweetest when you've known defeat."
— Malcolm S. Forbes

"Experience is the name every one gives to their mistakes."
— Oscar Wilde

"A goal is not always meant to be reached; it often serves simply as something to aim at."
— Bruce Lee

"If you wait to do everything until you're sure it's right, you'll probably never do much of anything."
— Win Borden

"Success is not the key to happiness. Happiness is the key to success. If you love what you are doing, you will be successful."
— Herman Cain

"I believe the last thing I read at night will likely manifest when I'm sleeping. You become what you think about the most."
— Daymond John

"The difference between school and life? In school, you're taught a lesson and then given a test. In life, you're given a test that teaches you a lesson."
— Tom Bodett

"To succeed in life, you need two things: ignorance and confidence."
— Mark Twain

"Be practical as well as generous in your ideals. Keep your eyes on the stars, but remember to keep your feet on the ground."
— Theodore Roosevelt

"For everything you have missed, you have gained something else, and for everything you gain, you lose something else."
— Ralph Waldo Emerson

"You have to learn the rules of the game. And then you have to play better than anyone else."
— Albert Einstein

"I do know that when I am 60, I should be attempting to achieve different personal goals than those which had priority at age 20."
— Warren Buffett

"One day your life will flash before your eyes. Make sure it's worth watching."
— Anonymous


"For success, attitude is equally as important as ability."
— Harry F. Banks


"You measure the size of the accomplishment by the obstacles you have to overcome to reach your goals."
— Booker T. Washington


"I put all my genius into my life; I put only my talent into my works."
— Oscar Wilde

"To succeed you need to find something to hold on to, something to motivate you, something to inspire you."
— Tony Dorsett

"You're always working to improve, and you're always being critiqued on your next performance. It's not about what you've done. There's always room to grow."
— Misty Copeland

"The most important things in life aren't things."
— Anthony J. D'Angelo

"Success means doing the best we can with what we have. Success is the doing, not the getting; in the trying, not the triumph. Success is a personal standard, reaching for the highest that is in us, becoming all that we can be."
— Zig Ziglar

"Some failure in life is inevitable. It is impossible to live without failing at something unless you live so cautiously that you might as well not have lived at all -- in which case, you fail by default."
— J.K. Rowling

"Risk, then, is not just part of life. It is life. The place between your comfort zone and your dream is where life takes place. It's the high-anxiety zone, but it's also where you discover who you are."
— Nick Vujicic

"Take up one idea. Make that one idea your life - think of it, dream of it, live on that idea. Let the brain, muscles, nerves, every part of your body, be full of that idea, and just leave every other idea alone. This is the way to success that is way great spiritual giants are produced."
— Swami Vivekananda


"There are no secrets to success. It is the result of preparation, hard work, and learning from failure."
— Colin Powell


"Never give up. Today is hard, tomorrow will be worse, but the day after tomorrow will be sunshine."
— Jack Ma

"Life is not measured by the number of breaths we take, but by the moments that take our breath away."
— Anonymous

"The road to success is always under construction."
— Lily Tomlin

"We think, mistakenly, that success is the result of the amount of time we put in at work, instead of the quality of time we put in."
— Arianna Huffington

"How wonderful it is that nobody need wait a single moment before starting to improve the world."
— Anne Frank

"Success is doing ordinary things extraordinarily well."
— Jim Rohn

"You don't learn to walk by following the rules. You learn by doing, and falling over."
— Richard Branson

"Life is the art of drawing without an eraser."
— John W. Gardner

"Success is going from failure to failure without losing enthusiasm."
— Winston Churchill

"The people who are crazy enough to think they can change the world are the ones who do."
— Steve Jobs

"Don't go through life, grow through life."
— Eric Butterworth

"For true success ask yourself these four questions: Why? Why not? Why not me? Why not now?"
— James Allen

"A person should set his goals as early as he can and devote all his energy and talent to getting there. With enough effort, he may achieve it. Or he may find something that is even more rewarding. But in the end, no matter what the outcome, he will know he has been alive."
— Walt Disney

"Life's challenges are not supposed to paralyze you; they're supposed to help you discover who you are."
— Bernice Johnson Reagon


"Your attitude, not your aptitude, will determine your altitude."
— Zig Ziglar


"The future rewards those who press on. I don't have time to feel sorry for myself. I don't have time to complain. I'm going to press on."
— Barack Obama


"I've learned that people will forget what you said, people will forget what you did, but people will never forget how you made them feel."
— Maya Angelou

"Success is not final; failure is not fatal: it is the courage to continue that counts."
— Winston Churchill


"To sit back and let fate play its hand out and never influence it is not the way man was meant to operate."
— John Glenn


"Life is 10% what happens to you and 90% how you react to it."
— Charles R. Swindoll


"Patience, persistence and perspiration make an unbeatable combination for success."
— Napoleon Hill

"If something is important enough, even if the odds are against you, you should still do it."
— Elon Musk


"I really don't think life is about the I-could-have-beens. Life is only about the I-tried-to-do. I don't mind the failure, but I can't imagine that I'd forgive myself if I didn't try."
— Nikki Giovanni


"Success is a science; if you have the conditions, you get the result."
— Oscar Wilde


"If you're not stubborn, you'll give up on experiments too soon. And if you're not flexible, you'll pound your head against the wall, and you won't see a different solution to a problem you're trying to solve."
— Jeff Bezos

"Life isn't about finding yourself. Life is about creating yourself."
— George Bernard Shaw

"The two most important requirements for major success are: first, being in the right place at the right time, and second, doing something about it."
— Ray Kroc

"Do the one thing you think you cannot do. Fail at it. Try again. Do better the second time. The only people who never tumble are those who never mount the high wire. This is your moment. Own it."
— Oprah Winfrey

"Live life so completely that when death comes to you like a thief in the night, there will be nothing left for him to steal."
— Anonymous


"Success builds character, failure reveals it."
— Dave Checkett


"The question I ask myself like almost every day is, 'Am I doing the most important thing I could be doing?'"
— Mark Zuckerberg


"If you live your life in the past, you waste the life you have to live."
— Jessica Cress

"Successful people aren't born that way. They become successful by establishing the habit of doing things unsuccessful people don't like to do. The successful people don't always like these things themselves; they just get on and do them."
— Anonymous

"I fear failure, but I won't let it stop me. Sometimes you just got to do it, or else it just doesn't happen."
— Mark Cuban

"The secret of health for both mind and body is not to mourn for the past, worry about the future, or anticipate troubles, but to live in the present moment wisely and earnestly."
— Buddha

"Success is 99 percent failure"
— Soichiro Honda


"Envision, create, and believe in your
own universe, and the universe will form
around you."
— Tony Hsieh


"Death is not the greatest loss in life.
The greatest loss is what dies inside us
while we live."
— Norman Cousins


"God doesn't require us to succeed; he
only requires that you try."
— Mother Teresa

"I think goals should never be easy;
they should force you to work, even if
they are uncomfortable at the time."
— Michael Phelps


"Success is not final; failure is not
fatal: it is the courage to continue that
counts."
— Winston Churchill


"The path to success is to take massive,
determined action."
— Anthony Robbins


"If you want to live a happy life, tie it
to a goal, not to people or things."
— Albert Einstein

"Be brave. Take risks. Nothing can substitute experience."
— Paulo Coelho


"Only as high as I reach can I grow, only as far as I seek can I go, only as deep as I look can I see, only as much as I dream can I be."
— Karen Ravn


"Everyone's dream can come true if you just stick to it and work hard."
— Serena Williams


"The best years of your life are the ones in which you decide your problems are your own. You do not blame them on your mother, the ecology, or the president. You realize that you control your own destiny."
— Albert Ellis

"Success is a state of mind. If you want success, start thinking of yourself as a success."
— Dr. Joyce Brothers


"It always seems impossible until it's done."
— Nelson Mandela


"We make a living by what we get, but we make a life by what we give."
— Winston Churchill


"Coming together is a beginning. Keeping together is progress. Working together is success."
— Henry Ford

"You can only become truly accomplished at something you love. Don't make money your goal. Instead, pursue the things you love doing, and then do them so well that people can't take their eyes off you."
— Maya Angelou

"Life is not meant to be easy, my child; but take courage -- it can be delightful."
— George Bernard Shaw

"Success seems to be connected with action. Successful people keep moving. They make mistakes, but they don't quit."
— Conrad Hilton

"I have not failed. I've just found 10,000 ways that won't work."
— Thomas Edison

"God, grant me the serenity to accept the things I cannot change, the courage to change the things I can, and the wisdom to know the difference."
— Reinhold Niebuhr

"Whatever you are, be a good one."
— Abraham Lincoln

"Obstacles are those frightful things you see when you take your eyes off your goal."
— Henry Ford

"Being deeply loved by someone gives you strength while loving someone deeply gives you courage."
— Lao Tzu

"Success is how high you bounce when you hit the bottom."
— General George S. Patton

"Instead of looking at the past, I put myself ahead twenty years and try to look at what I need to do now in order to get there then."
— Diana Ross

"A real friend is one who walks in when the rest of the world walks out."
— Walter Winchell

"You can only become truly accomplished at something you love. Don't make money your goal. Instead, pursue the things you love doing, and then do them so well that people can't take their eyes off you."
— Maya Angelou

"To win big, you sometimes have to take big risks."
— Bill Gates


"Nothing in life is to be feared. It is only to be understood."
— Marie Curie


"A successful man is one who can lay a firm foundation with the bricks others have thrown at him."
— David Brinkley


"Hustling is putting every minute and all your effort into achieving the goal at hand. Every minute needs to count."
— Gary Vaynerchuk

"Life isn't about having, it's about being. You could surround yourself with all that money can buy, and you'd still be as miserable as a human can be. I know people with perfect bodies who don't have half the happiness I've found. On my journeys, I've seen more joy in the slums of Mumbai and the orphanages of Africa than in wealthy gated communities and on sprawling estates worth millions. Why is that? You'll find contentment when your talents and passion are completely engaged, in full force. Recognize instant self-gratification for what it is. Resist the temptation to grab for material objects like the perfect house, the coolest clothes or the hottest car. Then if I just had X, I would be happy syndrome is a mass delusion. When you look for happiness in mere objects, they are never enough. Look around. Look within."
— Nick Vujicic

"Success always comes when preparation meets opportunity."
— Henry Hartman

"Learn how to be happy with what you have while you pursue what you want."
— Jim Rohn

"People of mediocre ability sometimes achieve outstanding success because they don't know when to quit. Most men succeed because they are determined to."
— George Allen

All you want to achieve is possible,
now all you need is to work hard and
Leave no stone unturned.
I wish you the best of luck on your
journey with the most inspiring lines
from Walter D. Wintle.

"If you think you are beaten, you
are.
If you think you dare not, you
don't.
If you'd like to win but think you
can't,
It's almost certain you won't.
Life's battles don't always go
To the stronger or faster man,
But sooner or later, the man who
wins
Is the man who thinks he can."

67161528R00025